ADRENALIN!
Diving
Paul Mason

Chrysalis Children's Books

First published in the UK in 2005 by
Chrysalis Children's Books
An imprint of the Chrysalis Books Group Plc
The Chrysalis Building, Bramley Road,
London W10 6SP

ISBN 1 84458 401 1

British Library Cataloguing in Publication Data for this book is available
from the British Library.

Associate Publisher Joyce Bentley
Senior editor Rasha Elsaeed
Project editors Jon Richards and Kate Simkins
Editorial assistant Camilla Lloyd
Designer Ed Simkins
Picture researcher Lorna Ainger
Consultant John Bantin

John became chief correspondent to Diver magazine in 1992 and continues to work as its technical
editor. He has travelled all around the world, photographing dive sites.

Produced by Tall Tree Ltd, UK

Printed in China

10 9 8 7 6 5 4 3 2 1

Typography Natascha Frensch
Read Regular, READ SMALLCAPS and Read Space; European Community Design Registration 2003
and Copyright © Natascha Frensch 2001-2004 Read Medium, **Read Black** and *Read Slanted*
Copyright © Natascha Frensch 2003-2004

READ™ is a revolutionary new typeface that will enhance children's understanding through clear,
easily recognisable character shapes. With its evenly spaced and carefully designed characters,
READ™ will help children at all stages to improve their literacy skills, and is ideal for young readers,
reluctant readers and especially children with dyslexia.

Disclaimer
In preparation of this book all due care has been exercised with regard to the advice, activities
and techniques depicted. The publishers regret that they can accept no liability for any loss or
injury sustained. When learning a new sport it is important to get expert tuition and to follow
any manufacturers' instructions.

Picture acknowledgments
All reasonable efforts have been made to ensure the reproduction of content has been done with
the consent of copyright owners. If you are aware of any unintentional omissions please contact
the publishers directly so that any necessary corrections may be made for future editions.
John Bantin: cover, 1, 3, 4, 5, 9–23, 25, 28–29
Corbis: 7, Tim Aylen/Reuters 27t, Bettmann 6b, 8, Jeffrey L Rotman 27b,
Bradley Smith 6t, Underwood and Underwood 26, Bill Varie 24
Digital Vision: 32

Contents

Underwater worlds

Diving is swimming underwater. Some divers just use a snorkel, while others carry tanks of air to breathe. Whatever the method, divers can explore a rich and diverse world, full of colourful creatures and fascinating wrecks.

The undersea realm

The world that lies beneath the ocean's surface is as varied as the one above. In tropical seas, giant coral reefs grow close to the surface and these are perfect for diving. The water is warm and brightly coloured fish are everywhere. Many divers visit these reefs on special holidays.

DIVING BRINGS YOU CLOSE TO SOME AMAZING SEALIFE.

Dive words

These are a few diving words that non-divers may not recognise.

BUDDY A diving partner.
FARMER JOHNS A type of wetsuit.
SPIKE DIVE Diving, then quickly coming back to the surface.
TURBIDITY Poor visibility in the water.

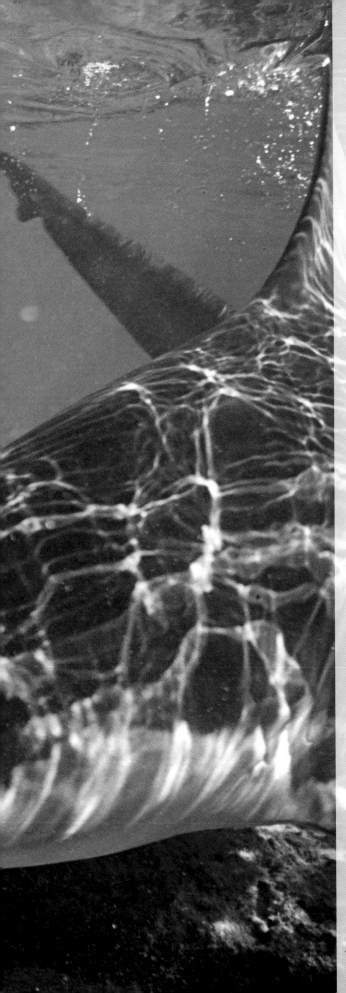

OUT OF THE WATER, DIVERS ARE WEIGHED DOWN BY LOTS OF HEAVY EQUIPMENT.

Daredevil divers

People have ventured into some very scary underwater places. Some have even explored under the frozen surface of the Arctic Ocean around the North Pole. They can only survive in the chilly water for a short time, so losing their way under the ice would be a disaster. The divers must be able to find their escape hole through the ice to get back to the surface. Cave diving is another daredevil diving activity. In this, divers explore undersea tunnels and cave systems. They worm their way through tiny spaces. Sometimes the divers can only fit through by taking off their air tanks and dragging them behind. Cave dives can be very long – the divers have to leave extra air tanks at key points, so that they do not run out of air.

Early underwater explorers

The first divers were people who simply held their breath before plunging under the sea. Ever since, people have developed better ways of exploring underwater.

Early divers

People have been diving in our seas for thousands of years. They were lured there by curiosity, the search for food or as a way of making a living. Ancient records speak of sponge divers, pearl divers, military divers and even salvage divers from 5000 years ago. Many early divers trained themselves to hold their breath for long periods of time. Over two minutes was common, but it is not as easy as it sounds. Most people begin to feel uncomfortable after about 15 or 20 seconds and have to take another breath after about 30 seconds – and that's without swimming down to the seabed and coming back up again.

THIS MODERN-DAY PEARL DIVER IS FROM JAPAN.

'Hard-hat' diving

In 1837, diving was revolutionised when Augustus Siebe invented the 'hard-hat' diving system. The hard-hat system pumped air into a large helmet. This allowed the diver to stay underwater far longer than before.

HARD-HAT DIVERS WORE HEAVY BOOTS AND BELTS SO THAT THEY COULD WALK ALONG THE SEABED. AIR WAS PUMPED INTO THE HELMET ALONG A RUBBER TUBE.

Recycling air

'Rebreathers' were invented in 1878. They re-use the gases a diver breathes out, turning them into breathable air. Rebreathers do not let out bubbles of air that could reveal a diver's location. During World War II (1939–45), Italian and British divers, or 'frogmen' as they were called, used them to attack enemy ships. Today, rebreathers have become popular with leisure divers because they allow them to spend more time underwater.

The human torpedoes

One method of underwater attack used by both British and Italian forces in World War II involved two frogmen riding on the back of a converted torpedo. Once beneath an enemy ship, the frogmen set a timer on the torpedo and swam away to safety. The torpedo would then explode and sink the ship.

THESE HUMAN TORPEDOES WERE NICKNAMED 'CHARIOTS' OR 'PIGS'.

Scuba diving

'Scuba' stands for 'Self-Contained Underwater Breathing Apparatus'. Scuba is the invention that first allowed ordinary people to roam freely under the sea. It is the main reason why diving is so popular today.

Regulating air

Modern scuba equipment was invented in 1943 by two Frenchmen, Jacques Cousteau and Emile Gagnan. Their system allowed divers to breathe air from tanks that they carried on their backs. The tanks contained compressed air. A device called a 'regulator' allowed the right amount of air to be released from the tanks and breathed in by the divers through their mouth.

COUSTEAU (CENTRE) DID A LOT OF WORK IN THE DEVELOPMENT OF UNDERWATER CAMERAS.

Scuba diving spreads

Cousteau later became a famous film-maker. His TV series *The Undersea World of Jacques Cousteau* was shown around the world. It told the story of the voyages of Jacques and his wife Mimi aboard their boat the *Calypso*. They explored different undersea areas, filming the habitats and sea creatures they saw. Today, we are used to seeing undersea pictures on our TV screens. Back then, very few people could imagine what it might be like to explore beneath the waves.

WITH THE HELP OF SCUBA GEAR, DIVERS CAN GET CLOSE TO CREATURES SUCH AS THIS GIANT GROUPER.

Diving today

Cousteau's work did much to make diving extremely popular. Today, thousands of divers explore underwater sites in places all around the world, from tropical reefs to frozen oceans.

THREE SCUBA DIVERS WALK OUT OF THE SEA HAVING JUST EXPLORED A TROPICAL REEF.

Dive gear

At its simplest, there is very little needed to go diving. You can go snorkelling in warm water with just some dive fins, a mask and a snorkel. However, scuba diving involves using quite a lot of equipment.

soft, wide sealing edge to mask

Seeing and breathing

All divers need to wear a mask to see underwater. A small tube, called a snorkel, can also be worn. This runs from the mouth and up the side of the head. The snorkel sticks out of the water when the diver's head is facing down and allows the diver to breathe.

material must not rot (silicone is popular)

strap adjuster

blade

adjustable straps

Some masks can be fitted with lenses to help people who wear glasses.

FINS HAVE DIFFERENT SIZES OF BLADES. THE LARGER THE BLADES, THE STRONGER YOUR LEG MUSCLES NEED TO BE.

Footwear

Fins, or flippers, are designed to help divers swim through the water easily and quickly. Some have an open heel with an adjustable strap, while others fit more like a shoe, covering the whole foot.

Air cylinders

The cylinders, or tanks, contain the compressed air that allows divers to breathe underwater. Steel cylinders are toughest, but they can rust and need a rubber 'tank boot' on their rounded bottoms to let them stand up. Aluminium cylinders are lighter and are flat-bottomed so they can be stood up without a tank boot. However, they scratch and dent more easily than steel. Divers breathe the air through a device called a 'regulator'.

nose pocket

Fully equipped

On a dive, divers will carry a lot of equipment. As well as air cylinders, mask, snorkel and fins, divers will wear a dive vest, also known as a 'buoyancy compensator' or 'BC'. Divers use this to move up and down in the water. They will also wear a wetsuit for warmth and a weight belt in order to sink to the bottom.

EVEN WITH ALL THIS EQUIPMENT, A DIVER WILL STILL APPEAR TO SWIM EFFORTLESSLY UNDERWATER.

The science of diving

Science plays an important part in diving. The equipment divers use was developed as a result of technological breakthroughs. Divers need to understand the science of how diving affects their bodies, as well as the scientific principles involved in life beneath the waves.

Floating underwater

Buoyancy is what allows divers to float in the water or to swim along without sinking or bobbing back up to the surface. A weight belt helps divers to sink. Once they reach the required depth, divers aim for 'neutral buoyancy' – neither sinking nor rising. They control their buoyancy using the buoyancy compensator. This vest can be filled with air from the tanks to make the diver more buoyant. A diver will let air out of the vest to sink and pump air into the vest to rise.

WITH THE HELP OF A BUOYANCY COMPENSATOR, DIVERS CAN HOVER AT WHATEVER DEPTH THEY WANT.

DIVING FACT

Divers going on a deep dive sometimes use helium gas instead of nitrogen to avoid nitrogen poison.

Under pressure

The air inside divers' tanks is compressed. This means that it is squeezed into the tanks under pressure, allowing more air to fit into them. Divers use this air to breathe and to fill their buoyancy compensators. In an emergency, the air can also be used to supply a fellow diver whose air has run out.

UNLESS A DIVER IS USING A REBREATHER, ANY AIR BREATHED OUT WILL RISE TO THE SURFACE AS BUBBLES.

Breathe easy

The correct mix of gases is vital to survival underwater and care needs to be taken when filling the air cylinders to get it right.

- Nitrogen forms about 78 per cent of air. It is absorbed by the body when under pressure during a dive. If too much nitrogen is absorbed, it can cause poisoning, called nitrogen narcosis.
- Oxygen forms about 21 per cent of air. It is vital for our survival underwater, but too much oxygen can be poisonous.

CYLINDERS ARE FITTED WITH HOSES HOLDING A GAUGE THAT SHOWS HOW MUCH AIR IS LEFT IN THE TANKS AND THE MOUTHPIECE.

13

Life underwater

The world beneath the waves is very different to the one above. Light and sound behave in different ways and, as warm-blooded creatures, we need to be careful that our bodies don't cool down too quickly.

Seeing underwater

Because water is more dense than air, light behaves differently beneath the waves. Objects seem to be about 25 per cent closer below the surface than they really are and look about 33 per cent bigger. Divers also need to be aware that there is less light the deeper they go. It becomes harder to see, and colours begin to disappear.

As a diver descends, fewer colours are visible and the underwater world becomes more drab.

Losing colour

Some colours of light cannot penetrate very far below the water's surface.

- Reds, oranges and yellows disappear at about 10 m.
- Greens last to about 20 m.
- After this, the only colours left are blues, which is why the deep sea often looks this colour.
- Finally, below about 35 m only greys remain.

Hearing

Sound travels very quickly underwater. This can make it hard to work out where a sound is coming from. On land, each of your ears hears a sound separately. The gap in time between one ear hearing it and then the other helps your brain to work out the sound's direction. Sound travels four times as fast through water as it does through air. It reaches both ears at almost the same time, making it difficult to work out where the sound came from.

MANY FISH, INCLUDING SHARKS, ARE EXTREMELY SENSITIVE TO UNDERWATER SOUNDS AND VIBRATIONS, ALLOWING THEM TO DETECT SOUNDS FROM SEVERAL KILOMETRES AWAY.

Feeling chilly

Divers lose heat underwater in several ways. The warmth in their breath is lost as they breathe out into the cooler water. Divers also lose heat through 'conduction' – that is, physical contact with the water. Water 'conducts' heat away from the body 25 times faster than air. This is why most divers wear a wetsuit. A wetsuit traps water next to the skin. This water is heated by the diver's body and provides an extra layer of insulation.

WETSUITS COME IN DIFFERENT STYLES. SOME COVER THE WHOLE BODY EXCEPT THE HEAD, HANDS AND FEET. OTHERS HAVE SHORTER ARMS AND LEGS FOR USE IN WARMER WATER.

Taking the plunge

Once people decide that they want to explore the undersea world, they need to go on a training course. The instructor will explain the safety procedures all divers must follow, the equipment they use and the different types of dive people go on.

Taking lessons

Many people first learn to dive by joining a club. Here, they can meet other people who are learning. The club may be able to lend them equipment, and the instructors will be experienced and well qualified. Finding a qualified instructor is very important however you learn to dive. Unqualified instructor may miss out important lessons or give incorrect advice.

A DIVER'S FIRST LESSONS WILL BE IN A SWIMMING POOL.

Intensive courses

Some people decide to learn to dive on an intensive course. These take about a week, with lots of training crammed in. One advantage of this is that divers earn their diving licences more quickly. Another is that the courses are often held in warm countries with clear water. This is great for people who live somewhere cold with murky water!

INTENSIVE COURSES SOMETIMES ALLOW DIVERS TO TRAIN IN OPEN WATER.

ONCE DIVERS HAVE THEIR C-CARDS, THEY CAN DIVE ANYWHERE IN THE WORLD.

Logs and cards

There are several important documents that a diver usually needs:

• Learner divers need to keep a 'dive log'. This is a record of their training dives.

• Once they have completed their training, they get a 'C-card' or 'certification card'.

• No one is allowed to go diving without a C-card, and dive shops will not fill air tanks without one being shown.

Underwater techniques

There are many skills that a diver needs to learn, from the correct way to enter the water to a whole language of hand signals that allows divers to communicate with each other underwater.

Jump in!

There are fours basic ways of getting into the water. Divers going into the water from a beach wade in backwards. From a boat or the side of a pool, divers can twist in from a sitting-down position. Or they can jump in feet-first, either with their feet together or by taking a giant step. Finally, they can do a backwards roll into the water.

DIVERS HOLD ON TO THEIR FACE MASKS AS THEY JUMP IN.

Diving hand language

These are some of the basic signals divers use to communicate with each other underwater:

1. Let's descend.
2. Let's go back to the surface or go up.
3. I have no more air.
4. Are you OK? I am OK.

Seeing clearly

All divers have to know how to clear their mask of water in case it leaks or is knocked off. They push lightly on the top of the mask and breathe out gently through their nose. The mask fills with air, and the water is driven out of the bottom. Some masks have a 'purge valve' – a special device for clearing them. With these masks, divers just have to tilt their head down and breathe out.

IF A MASK FILLS WITH WATER THE DIVER WILL BE UNABLE TO SEE.

Painful pressure

While descending, divers need to 'clear' their ears – otherwise increasing pressure can cause pain. To do this, they will use one of the techniques explained on the right.

Clearing the ears

TOYNBEE TECHNIQUE	Hold the nose, close the mouth and swallow.
VALSALVA TECHNIQUE	Hold the nose, close the mouth and gently try to breathe out.

Buddy diving

Once underwater, divers work in pairs so that if one of them gets into trouble, the other can help out. This is called the buddy system.

Snorkelling

Divers on the surface use their snorkel to save the air in their tanks. Simple snorkelling is great fun, and many people start diving in this way. During a dive to the bottom, the snorkel fills with water. Back on the surface it needs to be cleared with a strong blow of air, before the diver can breathe through it again.

THE DIVER ON THE RIGHT IS FORCING WATER OUT OF HIS SNORKEL BY EXHALING.

DIVING FACT

If two buddies become separated during a dive, they should only spend one minute looking for each other before abandoning the dive and returning to the surface.

Underwater navigation

Buddies always agree on a direction to follow while they are underwater. This makes it less likely that they will become separated. Many divers use a compass to keep track of the direction they are moving. This also makes it less likely that they will swim too far from their diveboat.

IF ONE OF THE BUDDIES RUNS OUT OF AIR, THEY WILL NEED TO SHARE, EITHER BY TAKING TURNS TO BREATHE THROUGH ONE MOUTHPIECE OR BY USING A SPARE. THIS IS CALLED 'BUDDY BREATHING'.

Head-to-toe buddy check

Diving buddies do these checks on each other before they start a dive, to make sure they have the right equipment and that it's working.

- mask in place.
- snorkel attached.
- scuba tank secure and valve open.
- SPG (Submersible Pressure Gauge) OK.
- regulator OK, working with main and back-up air sources.
- buoyancy compensator OK.

- weights in place, release system working.
- wetsuit properly zipped.
- knife safely stored.
- fins on securely.
- dive watch, timer or computer working – timing a dive is crucial so that divers do not stay underwater for too long.

Diving safety

There are dangerous creatures in the sea, such as jellyfish, snakes, sharks and eels. However, people are more likely to be hit by a car while crossing the street than a diver being hurt by a sea creature. The biggest danger is from the sea itself.

Powerful forces

Currents and tides can funnel through a narrow opening or into a cave. If caught in them, a diver could be pinned down under the surface. Divers can also be carried away from their diveboat by currents. In 2004, for example, some divers in the Red Sea were swept away from their boat. They were only rescued after spending hours drifting in the water.

THIS DIVER IS HOLDING AN INFLATABLE SIGNALLING DEVICE. IF DIVERS ARE CARRIED A LONG WAY FROM THEIR DIVEBOAT BY CURRENTS, THEY CAN INFLATE THIS DEVICE USING AIR FROM THEIR TANKS. IT STICKS OUT OF THE WATER AND CAN BE SEEN CLEARLY FROM FAR AWAY.

Rising too quickly

Decompression sickness (DCS) happens when divers come to the surface too quickly. Their body is unable to adjust to the change in pressure between deep water and the surface. DCS has to be treated quickly or it gets worse and can even cause death. People suffering from DCS are put inside a recompression chamber. This puts the same pressure on their body as they experienced under the sea.

ONCE INSIDE A RECOMPRESSION CHAMBER, THE PRESSURE IS SLOWLY INCREASED BACK TO NORMAL.

Getting stuck

Becoming entangled below the surface is extremely dangerous, as a diver's air will soon run out. Divers need to take extra care when exploring wrecks or areas where they can become entangled with underwater plants, such as seaweed, and obstacles, such as nets.

DIVERS SHOULD ALWAYS CARRY KNIVES IN ORDER TO CUT THEMSELVES FREE FROM OBSTACLES.

Decompression sickness symptoms

- skin rash.
- numbness and weakness.
- tingling feelings.
- paralysis.

Fit to dive

You do not have to be a super-athlete to be a diver. Just a good level of normal fitness is fine, although you must be able to swim. It is more important to be comfortable in the water than to be a fast swimmer.

Diving requirements

At the start of a diving course, people usually take a swimming test. Normally, they need to be able to swim 200 m without stopping and swim about 8 m underwater without a push-off. By the end of the course, these distances are increased to 300 m and 15 m. Some people with asthma, diabetes or physical disabilities can dive but should speak to their doctor first. People who suffer from epilepsy cannot go diving.

SOME DIVERS FIND THAT SWIMMING INCREASES THEIR LUNG CAPACITY AND HELPS WITH THEIR UNDERWATER BREATHING.

DIVING FACT

It is not a good idea to eat just before a dive. Eating diverts blood to the stomach, which can cause painful cramps in your muscles.

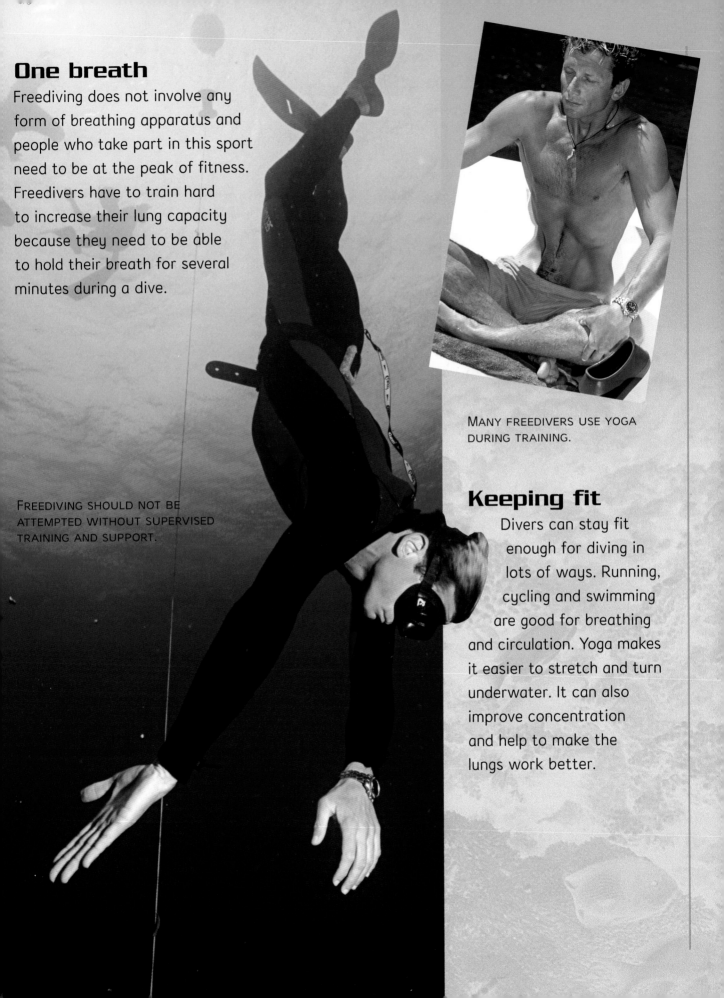

One breath

Freediving does not involve any form of breathing apparatus and people who take part in this sport need to be at the peak of fitness. Freedivers have to train hard to increase their lung capacity because they need to be able to hold their breath for several minutes during a dive.

MANY FREEDIVERS USE YOGA DURING TRAINING.

FREEDIVING SHOULD NOT BE ATTEMPTED WITHOUT SUPERVISED TRAINING AND SUPPORT.

Keeping fit

Divers can stay fit enough for diving in lots of ways. Running, cycling and swimming are good for breathing and circulation. Yoga makes it easier to stretch and turn underwater. It can also improve concentration and help to make the lungs work better.

Famous divers

Diving is not usually a competitive sport, but even without Olympic champions there are still plenty of famous divers who are known around the world. However, freediving is competitive – freedivers try to see who can go the deepest on a single breath.

Underwater pioneer

Frenchman Jacques Cousteau was a diving pioneer, inventor, explorer, scientist and film-maker. His films did more than anything else to make diving popular. Cousteau was passionate about preserving the underwater environment and set up the Cousteau Society to protect the sea from damage by people.

Hans Haas

A famous Austrian diver and photographer, Haas was one of the first people to take successful underwater photos. His pictures of the Maldives, for example, made divers around the world realise how great the diving was there.

JACQUES COUSTEAU PREPARES TO SUBMERGE IN A SHARK CAGE TO FILM THESE UNDERWATER PREDATORS.

Freediving champ

Tanya Streeter set her first world record in 1998, just a few months after taking up the sport of freediving.

BORN	Grand Cayman, Caribbean, 1972
HEIGHT	1.75 m
WEIGHT	73 kg
WORLD RECORDS	'Absolute' records set in 2003, 2002, 1999 and 1998. Eight world records broken in total.
CAREER FACTS	The world's most famous freediver, Tanya is one of the few female athletes able to take on and beat the men, setting 'absolute' world records in the process.

STAN HAS WON FIVE EMMY AWARDS FOR HIS UNDERWATER FILMS.

Film-maker

Stan Waterman first began diving in Florida in 1936 using just a Japanese diver's mask. He is now a famous underwater film-maker. Stan's most famous film is probably *Blue Water, White Death* (1968) about great white sharks. Peter Benchley, the author of *Jaws*, is said to have used this film as inspiration for his book.

Great dive sites

Divers have explored the shallow seas that surround almost all the world's lands. Nearly every coast has groups of keen divers who spend their free time diving on wrecks, reefs, rocks or other places.

Islands, reefs and wrecks

The Caribbean Sea is dotted with small islands. These are perfect waters for divers. The sea is warm and the coral reefs, wrecks and fish are plentiful. Among the favourite diving places are the Bahamas, Bonaire, the Virgin Islands, the Cayman Islands and Cozumel.

A DIVER PHOTOGRAPHS A SHARK IN THE SEAS OFF THE BAHAMAS.

Scapa Flow

LOCATION	Scapa Flow, off the Scottish island of Orkney.
DESCRIPTION	A natural harbour where there are many giant wrecks for divers to explore.
HISTORY	On 21 June 1919, the German fleet was scuttled at Scapa Flow – 52 ships sank, though 45 of these were later raised.
ATTRACTIONS	Seven remaining wrecked warships are still there, plus a World War II U-boat.

The Great Barrier Reef

One of the most famous diving locations in the world, the Great Barrier Reef lies off the northeast coast of Australia. The reef stretches in a broken chain of more than 2000 km. Its oldest parts are about 500 000 years old.

A CUTTLEFISH HOVERS OVER THE CORAL OF THE GREAT BARRIER REEF.

Warm paradise

The Red Sea lies between Africa and the Middle East. Its coasts are home to many favourite dive sites. The area is famous for its clear, warm waters that allow divers to see for up to 50 m. The variety of undersea sights includes coral reefs, wrecks and the famous offshore islands known as The Brothers.

Galapagos

Divers are attracted to the Galapagos Islands off South America because of the rich diversity of marine life. It includes sea turtles, manta rays, dolphins, sea lions, penguins and sharks.

A DIVER APPROACHES A HUGE WHALE SHARK OFF THE GALAPAGOS ISLANDS.

Diving words

blade The flat part of a fin that pushes against the water to cause movement.

buddy A diving partner. Diving buddies rely on each other for help if something goes wrong underwater.

circulation The movement of blood around the body.

compressed air The air in divers air tanks. It is forced into the tanks under high pressure. This means more air can fit into the tanks, allowing divers to stay underwater for longer.

coral A stony material formed of the skeletons of many tiny marine animals. Usually found in tropical seas.

cylinder Another name for 'tank'.

farmer johns A type of wetsuit that fastens over the diver's shoulder.

frogmen An old-fashioned name for divers, especially military divers.

insulation Something that stops the movement or loss of heat.

numbness Loss of feeling in parts of the body.

open-water dive A dive that takes place outside a swimming pool, usually in the sea, a lake or a river.

paralysis Not being able to move.

pressure A force, such as the weight of water, pressing against a surface.

reef A ridge of coral, sand or rock near to the surface of the sea, often along a coast or around an island.

regulator The device that allows divers to breathe in air from their air tanks while underwater, then breathe it back out again.

salvage Something rescued from a disaster, for example, goods rescued from a sunken ship.

scuttled Deliberately sunk.

snorkel A pipe that curves from the mouth up to the surface, allowing divers to breathe with their faces underwater.

SPG Short for 'Submersible Pressure Gauge', a device that shows divers how much air is left in their tanks.

spike dive Diving, then quickly coming back to the surface.

tank The metal container that holds the air that divers breathe underwater.

tropical Describes areas that lie either side of the Equator, the imaginary line that runs around the middle of the Earth's surface. The 'tropics' are the regions between the lines called the Tropic of Cancer in the north and the Tropic of Capricorn in the south. These areas are known for their warm climates.

turbidity Poor visibility in the water, usually caused by mud or sand being stirred up.

yoga A form of exercise that involves putting the body into various positions that strengthen the muscles and make the joints more flexible.

Films

The Big Blue (1998)
French film that tells the story of a band of freedivers who compete against each other to achieve the deepest dive.
Open Water (2004)
The story of a couple of divers who are left by their diveboat in shark-infested waters.

Books to read

Scuba Diving: The Essential Guide to Equipment and Techniques by Jack Jackson (New Holland, 2004)
Dive Atlas of the World: An Illustrated Reference to the Best Sites by Jack Jackson (ed.) (The Lyons Press, 2003)
The Diver's Handbook by Alan Mountain (The Lyons Press, 1997)

Magazines

There are several magazines published for divers. In the UK, there are *Dive* magazine and *Diver*. Both cover the latest developments in diving and the best locations to visit. *Sport Diver Interactive* (www.sportdiver.com) is the official publication of the PADI Diving Society and offers reviews of dive sites around the world and equipment.

Further information

British Sub-Aqua Club
www.bsac.com
Telford's Quay,
South Pier Road,
Ellesmere Port,
Cheshire CH65 4FL
United Kingdom

Index